FAT LADIES IN SPAAAAACE
a body-positive coloring book

drawn and written by
Nicole Lorenz

ISBN 978-1463786830

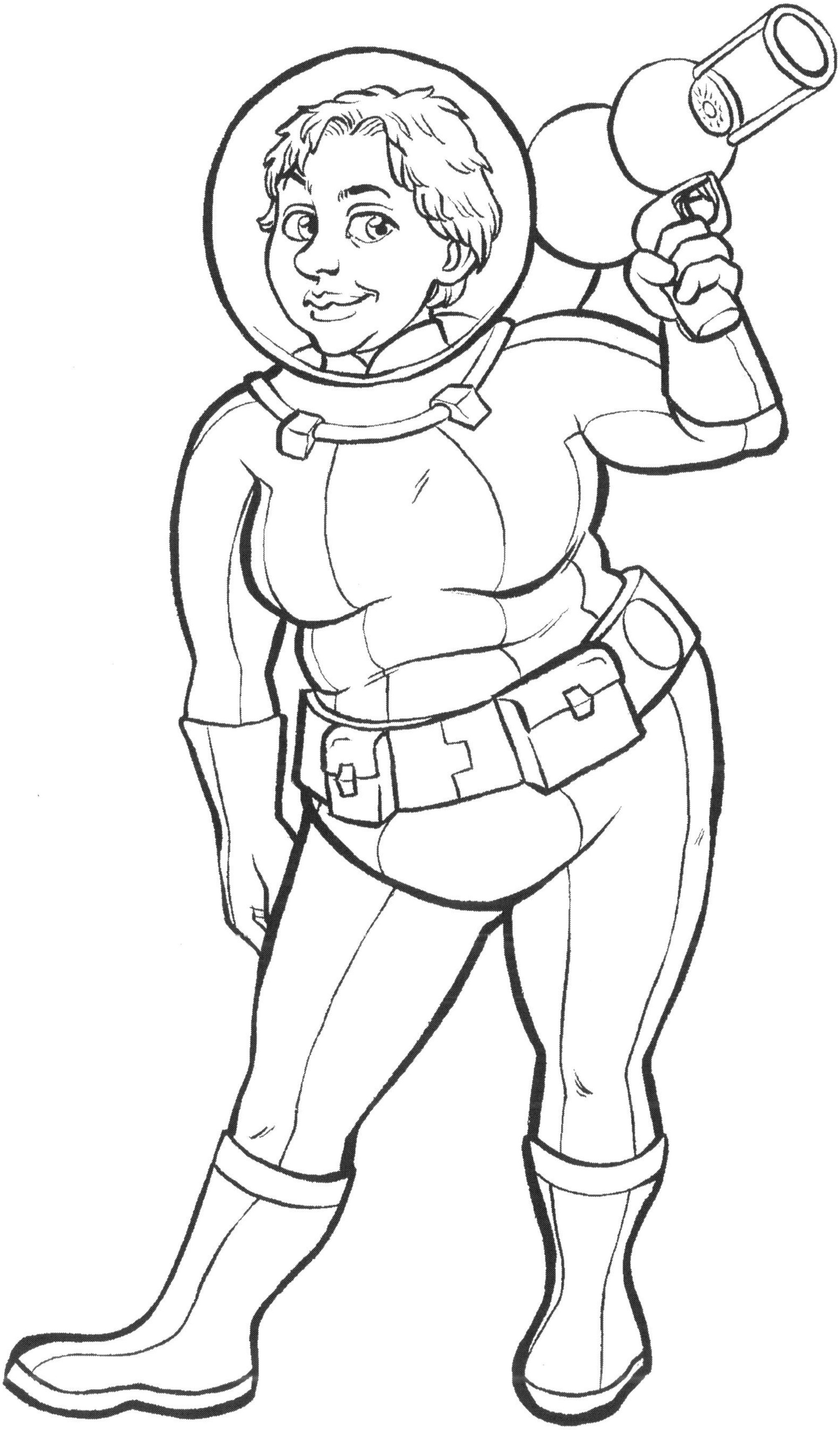

Sincerity explores the edges of the universe, charting new planets and seducing alien women.

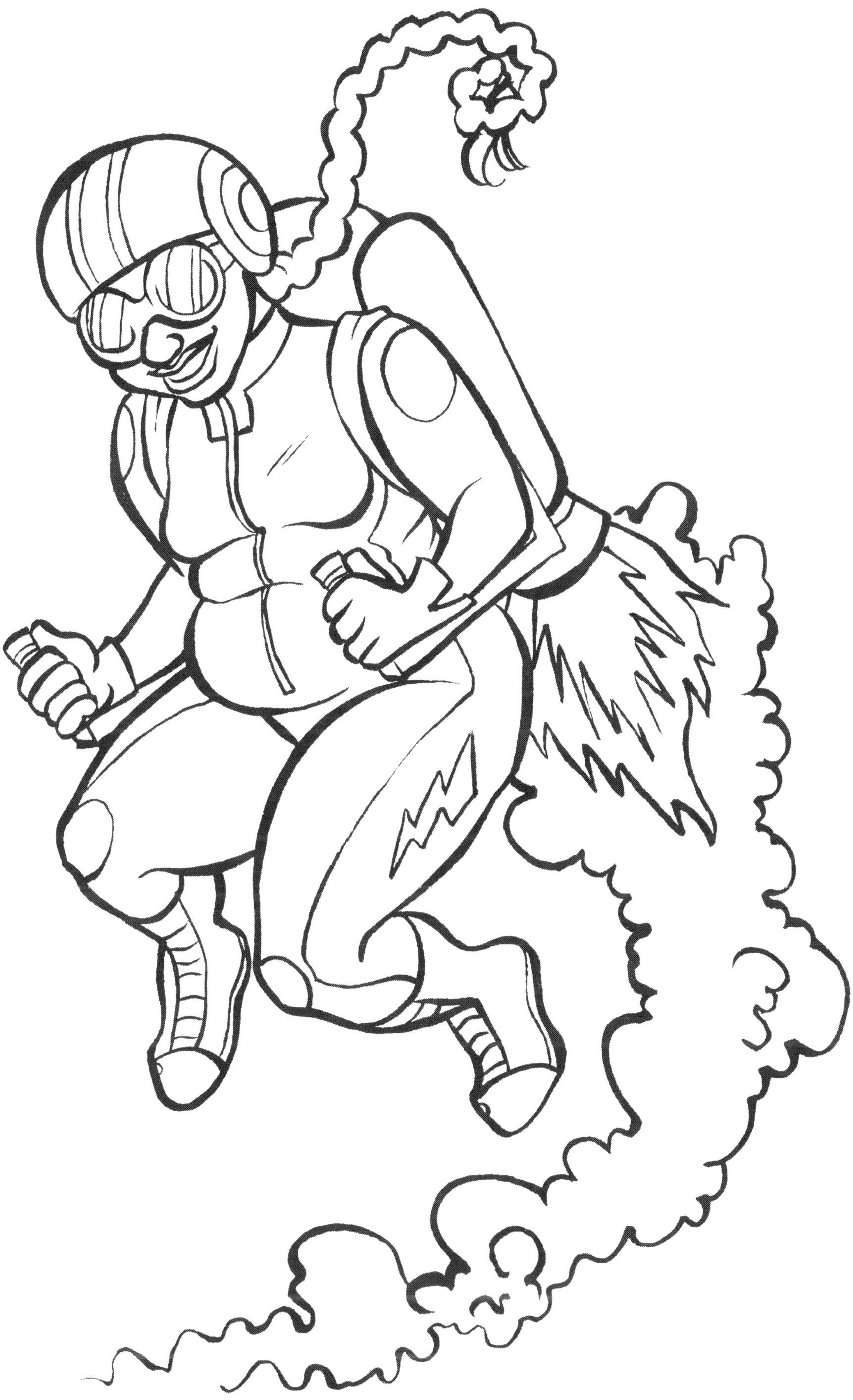

As a rocketeer, Pepin scoffs at gravity!
(Scoffing at gravity is in the job requirements.)

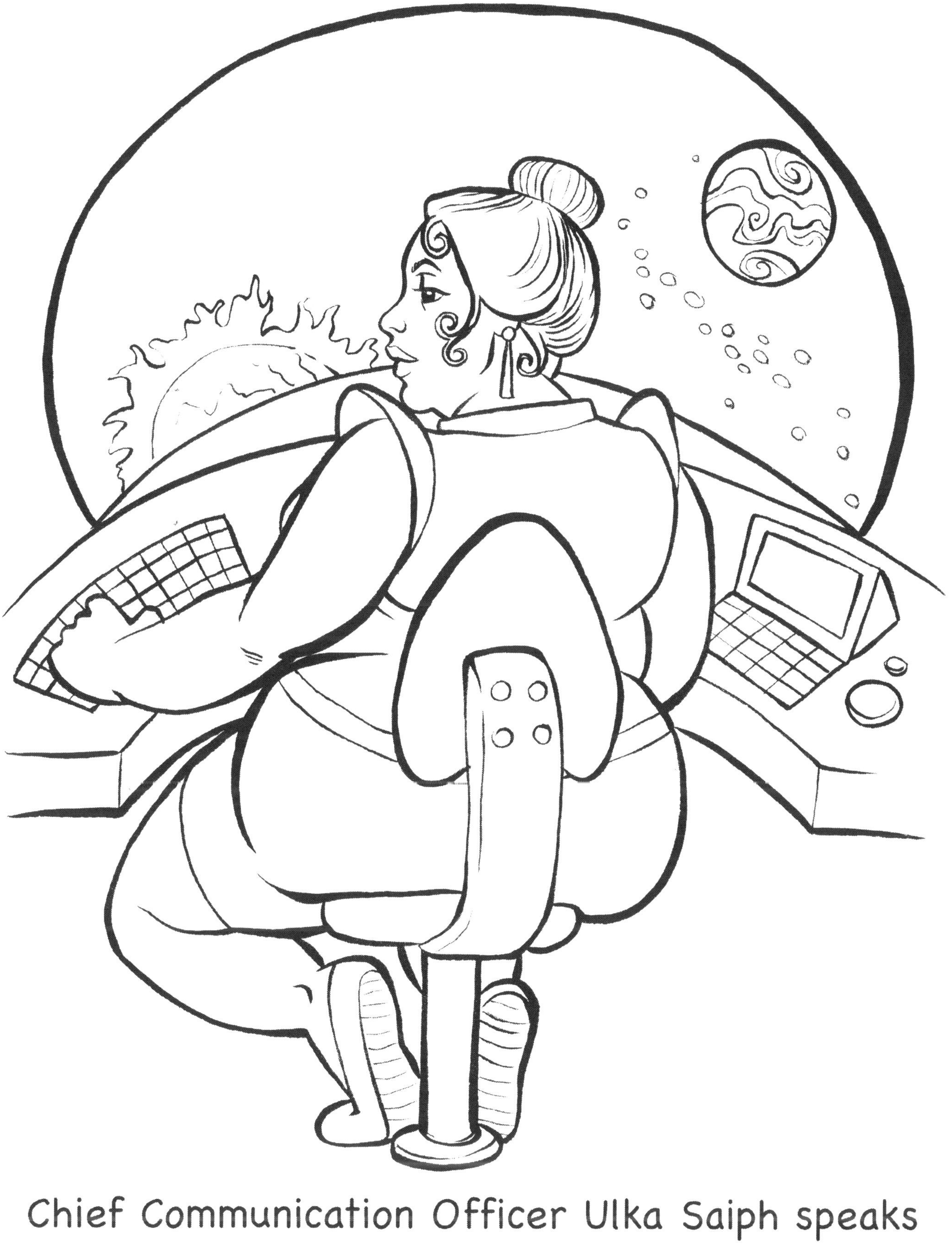

Chief Communication Officer Ulka Saiph speaks seventeen languages from across three galaxies and knows how to swear in five more.

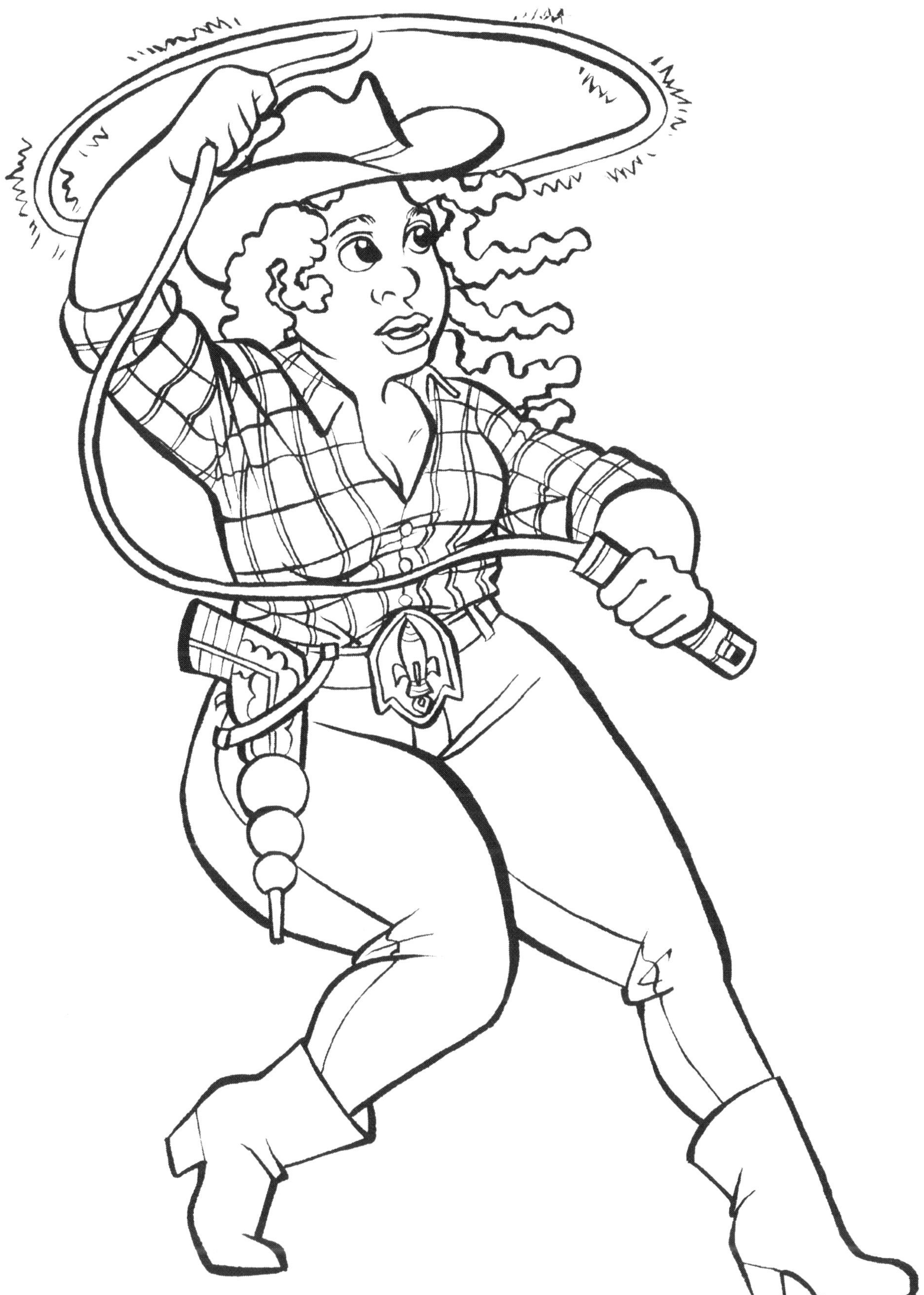

Joanna Beθ is set to inherit her family's cattle ranch on Persephone when her parents retire to Io.

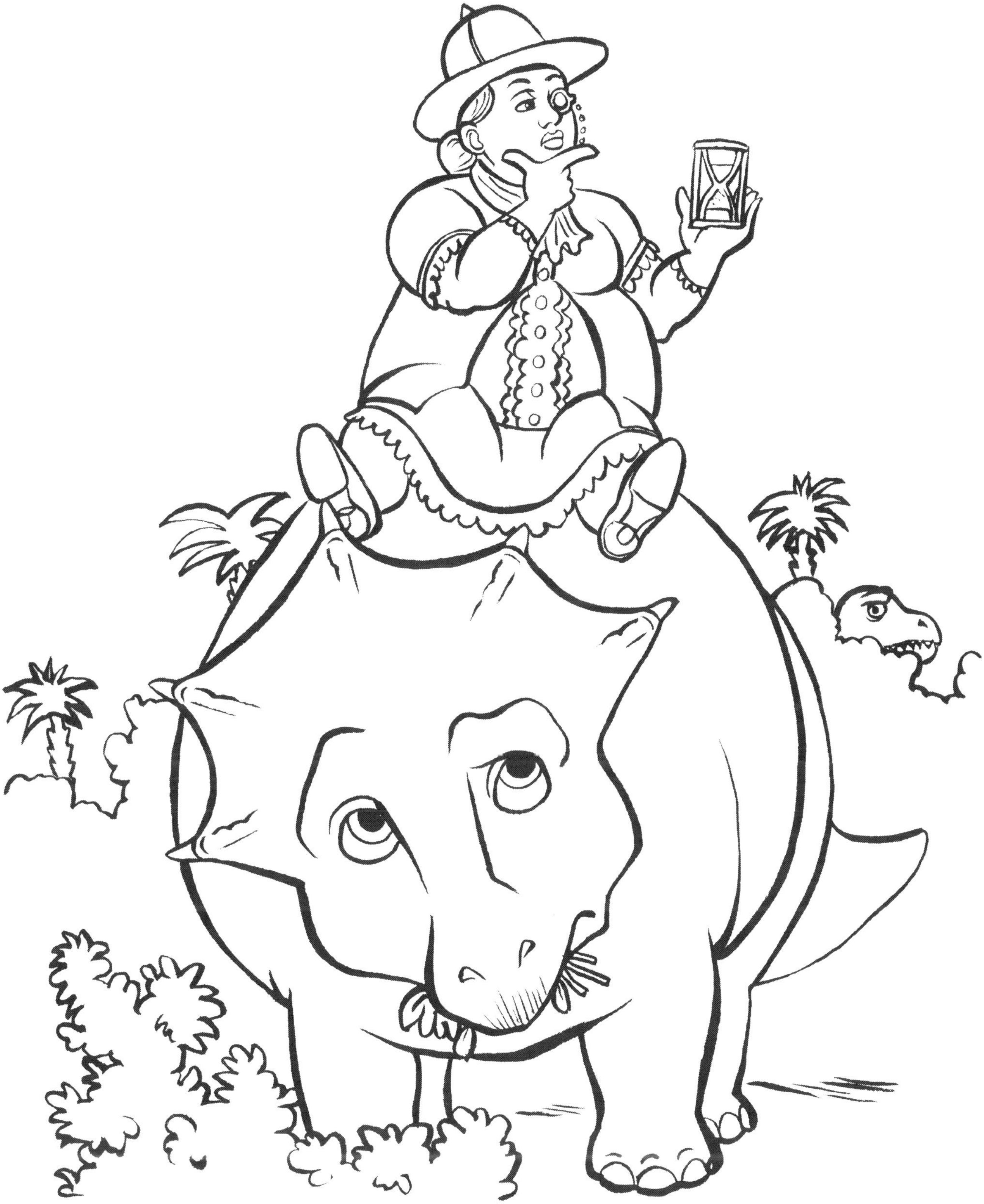

The Time Device is never perfectly accurate,
but Cybil Ellingworth IV is annoyed to have overshot
the Defenestration of Prague by quite this wide a margin.

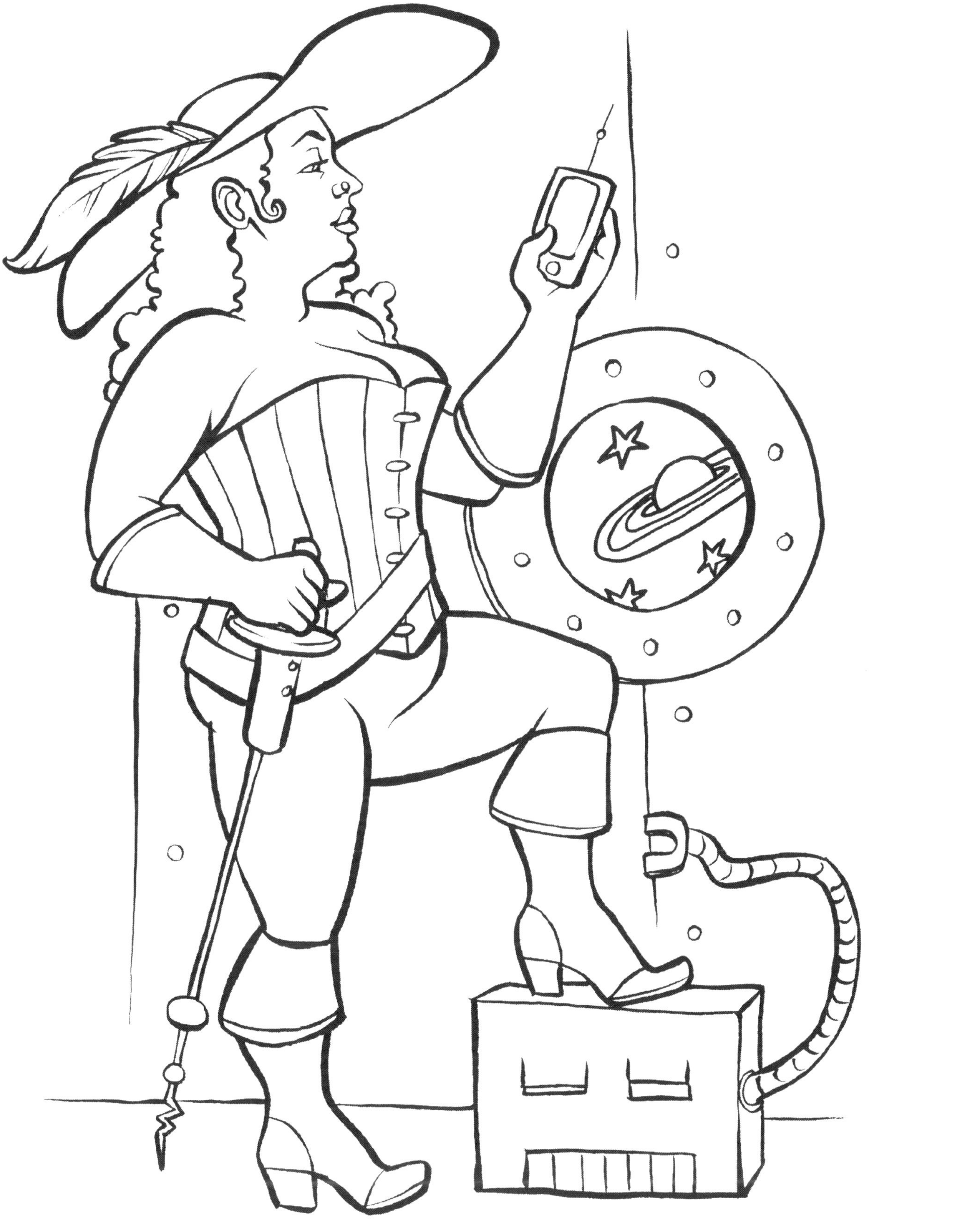

The name Valentina "The Bloody Nova" Rackham strikes terror into hearts, hemocoels, and hard drives throughout Sector R19.

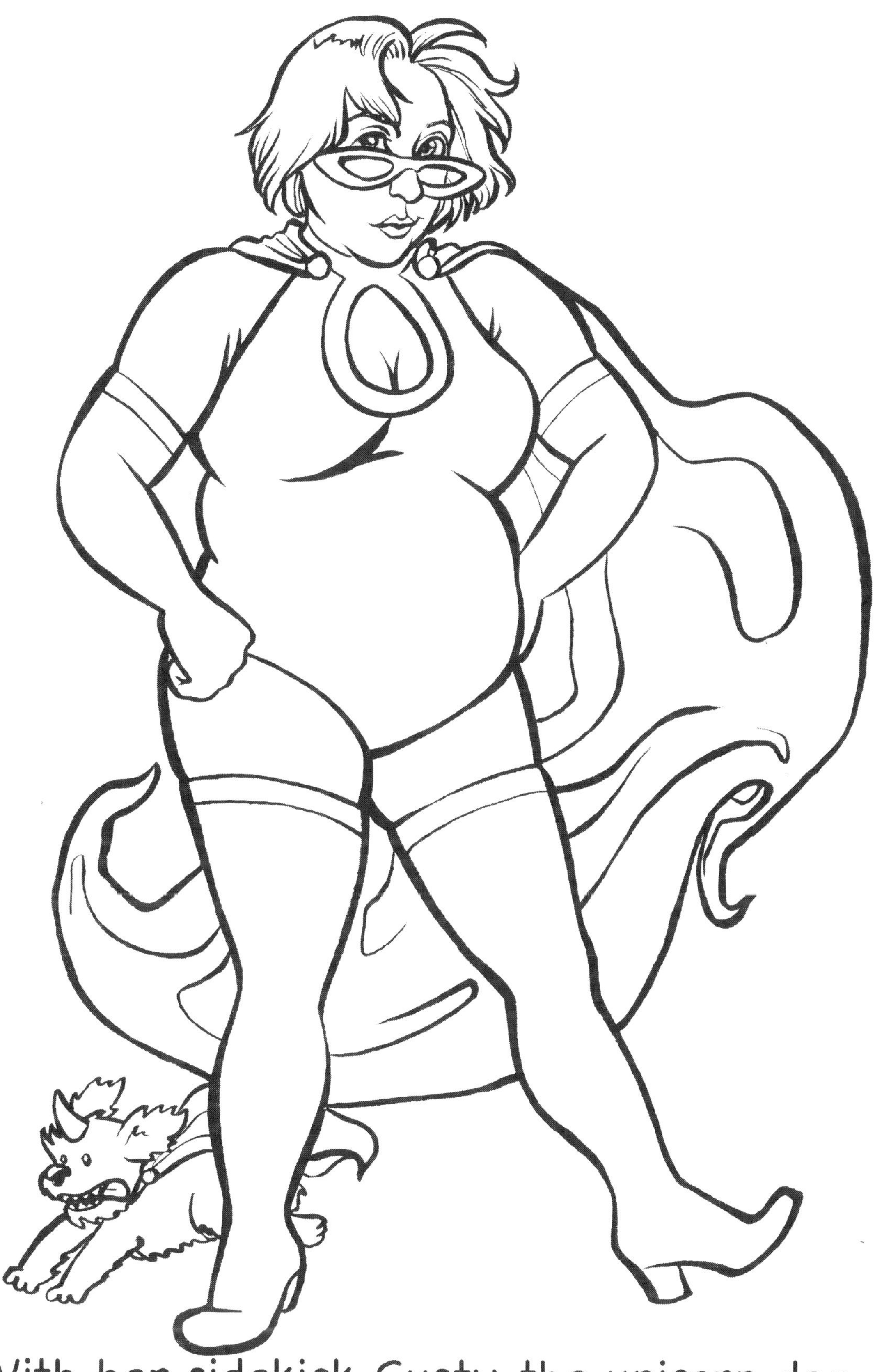

With her sidekick Gusty the unicorn dog,
The Zaftig Zephyr spends her nights protecting
the rain-spattered streets of Metrolopolis.

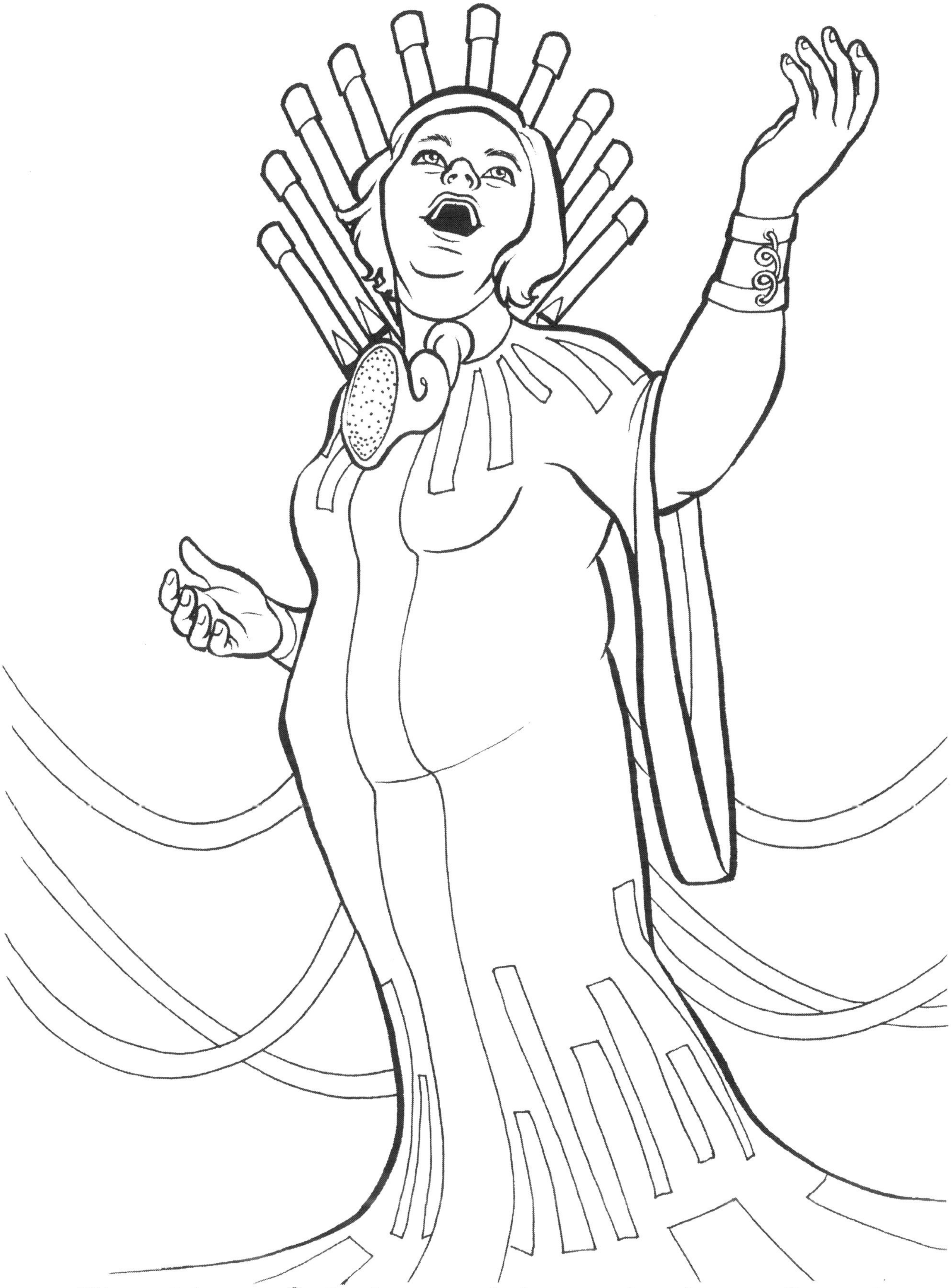

The Diva of Orion got her start performing covers of Top 40 hits with her high school glee club.

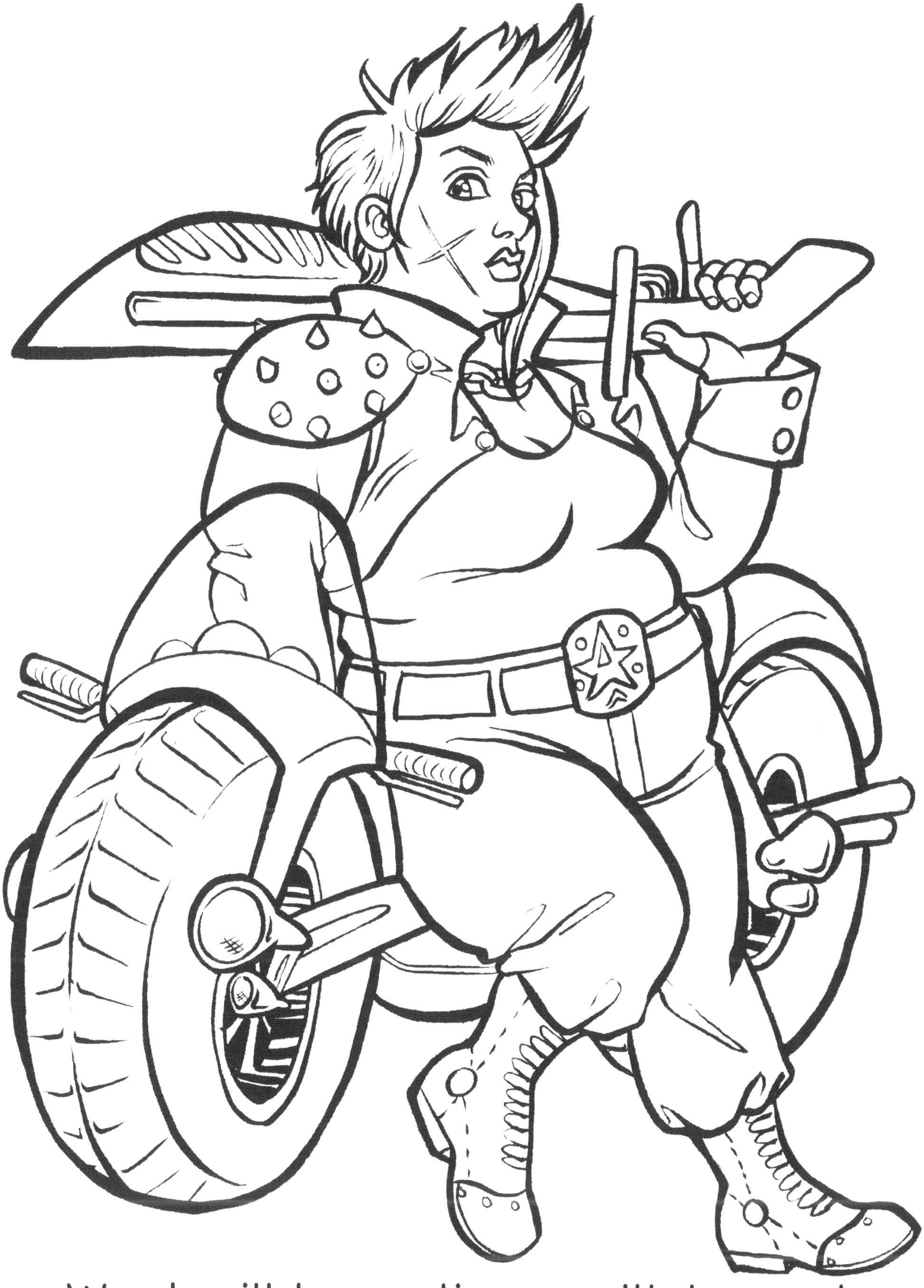

Wreck will be meeting up with her party
after this motorcycle chase cutscene.

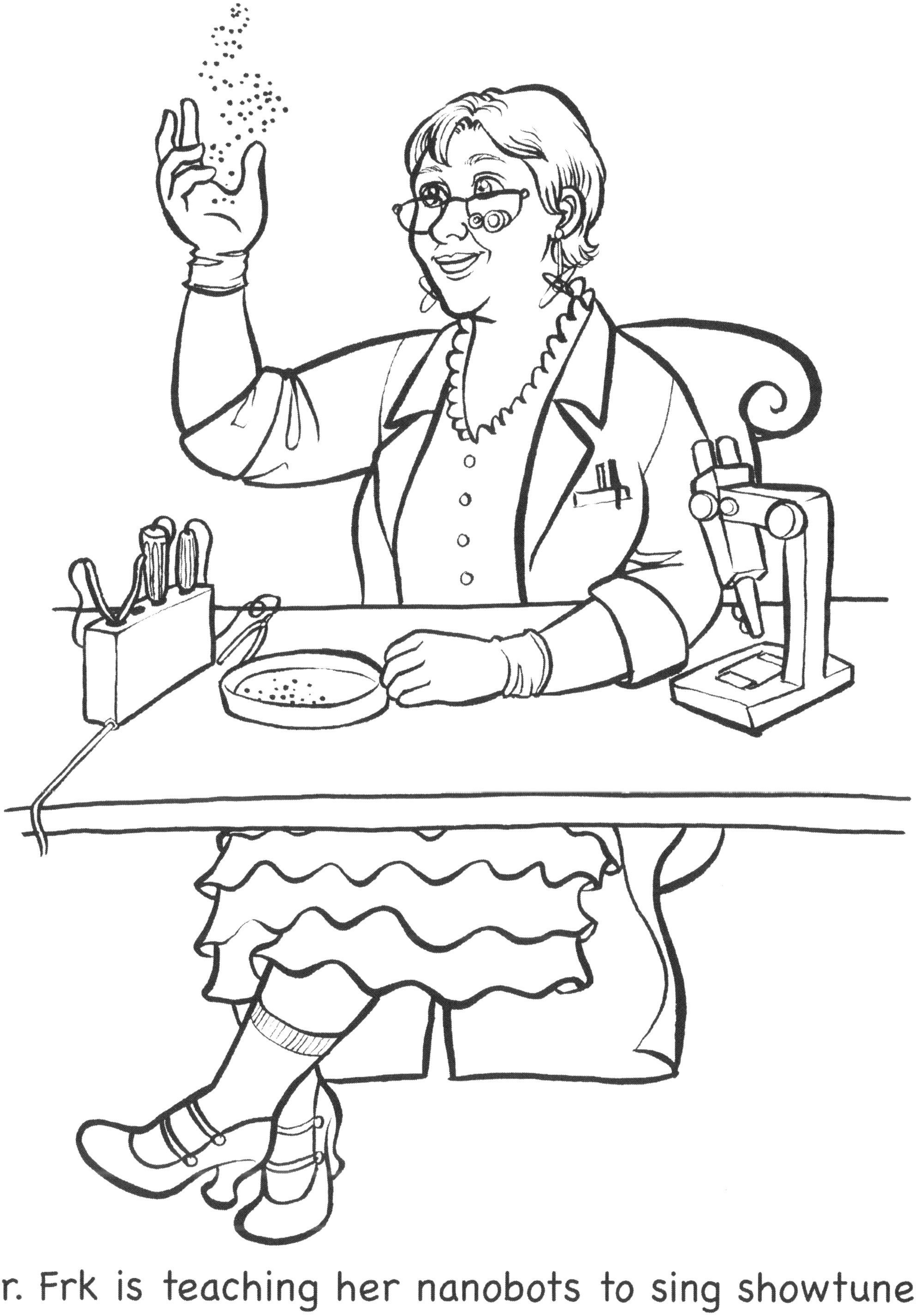

Dr. Frk is teaching her nanobots to sing showtunes.

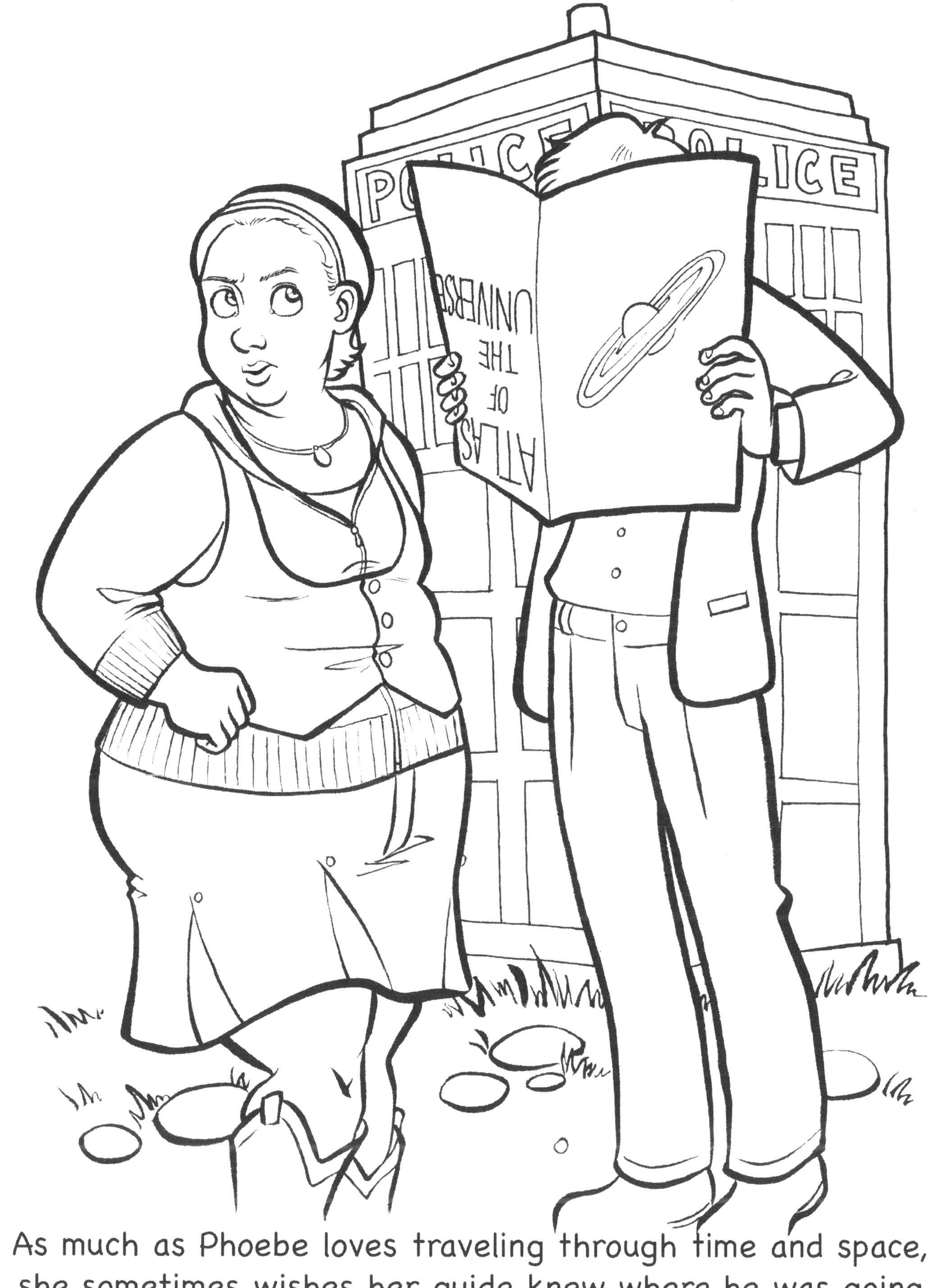
POLICE
POLICE
ATLAS OF THE UNIVERSE

As much as Phoebe loves traveling through time and space, she sometimes wishes her guide knew where he was going.

When none of her friends are online, Jeneva uses her cerebral LINK connection to download country music.

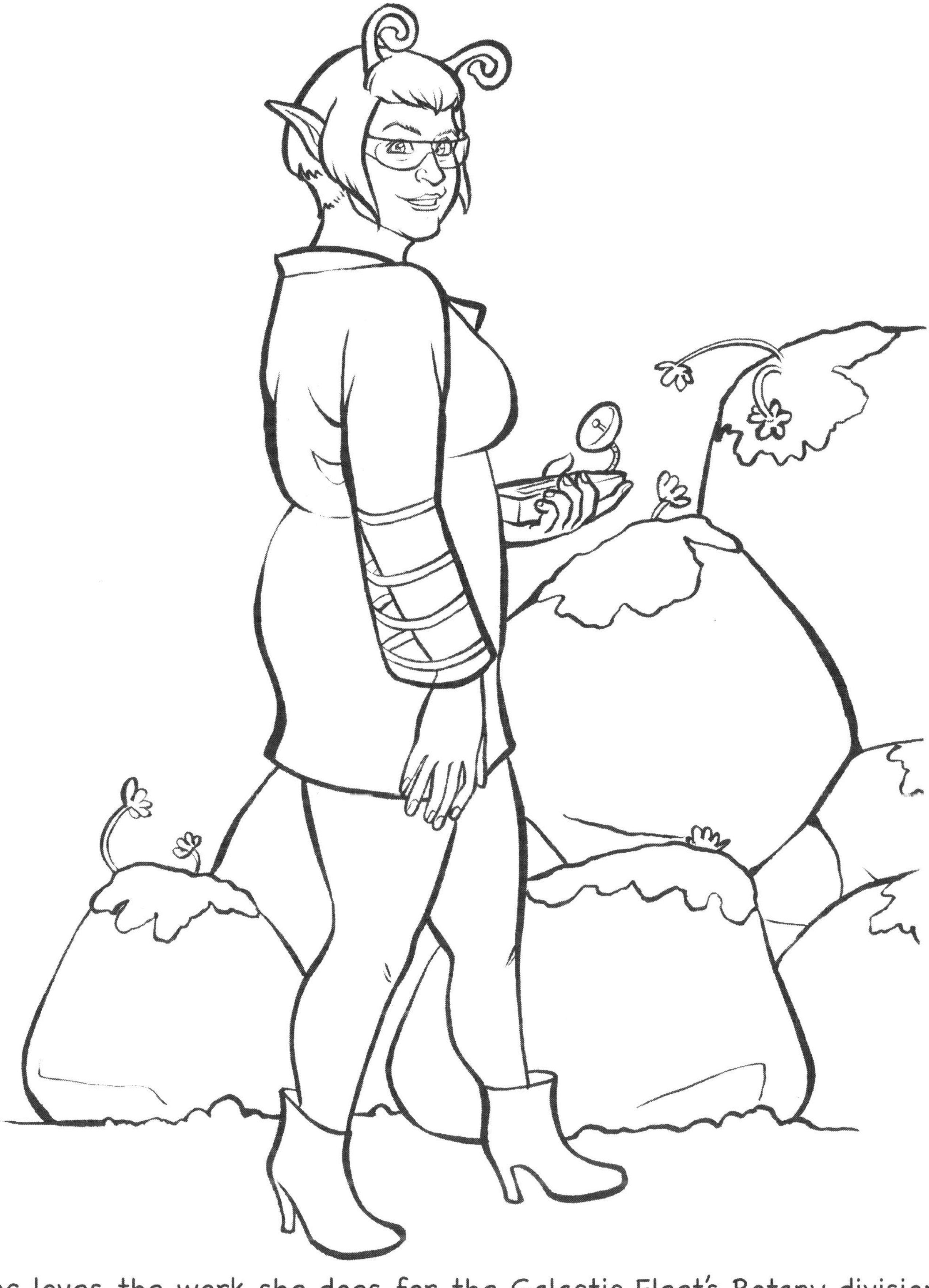

Bec loves the work she does for the Galactic Fleet's Botany division.
Her arctic home planet is too cold for plants - or for mini-dresses.

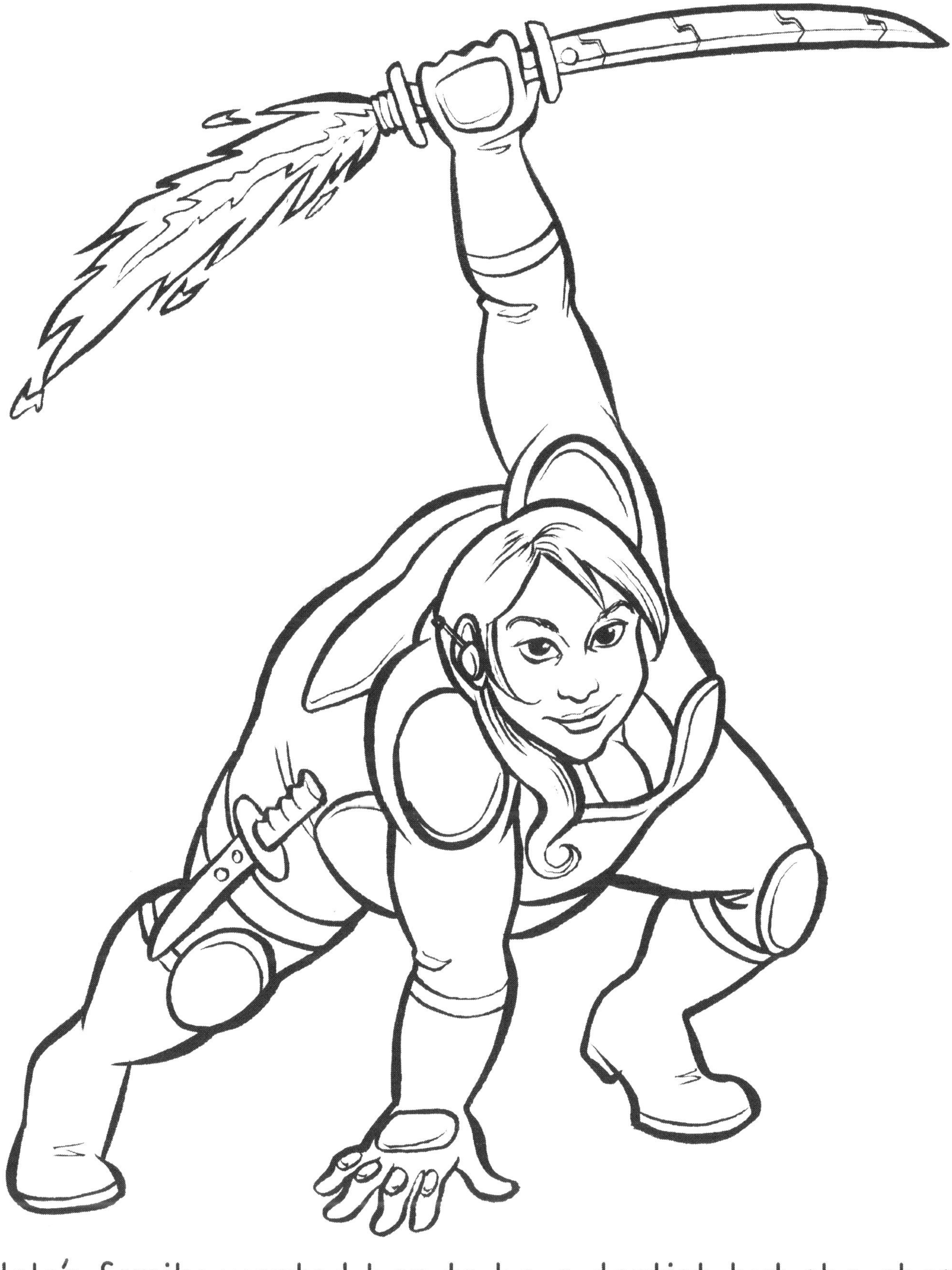

Adele's family wanted her to be a dentist, but she chose to join the elite bodyguard forces of the Space Pope.

Dolly thinks the masseurs on the **last** intergalactic cruise she took
were better, but she supposes they can't all be six-armed Crustaceans.

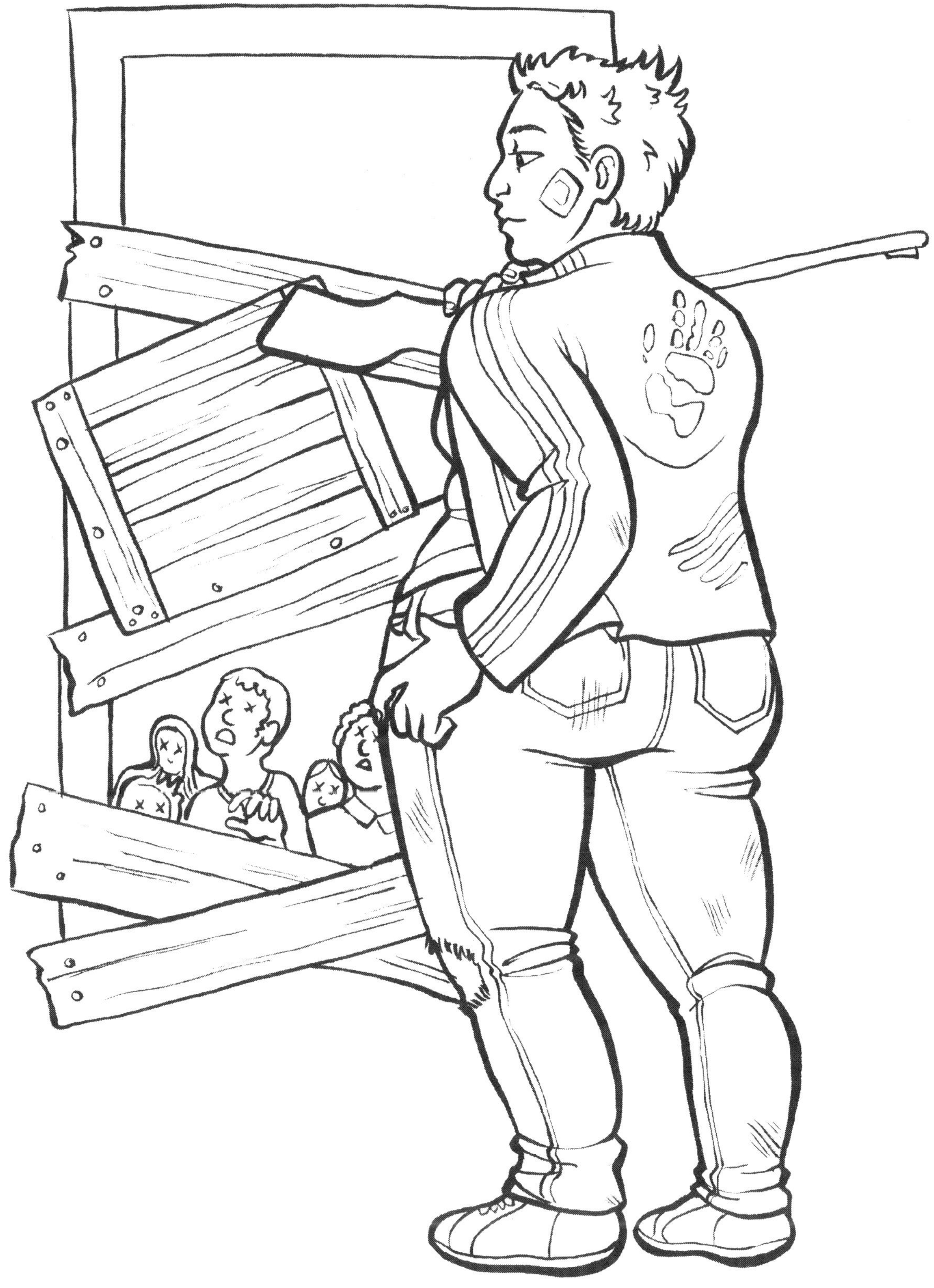

Zero's been hunting zombies since before you were turned, bub.
She ain't falling for your "Knock, knock, pizza delivery" trick.

Blackthorn-862 was genetically engineered
to be the perfect assassin and cocktail party guest.

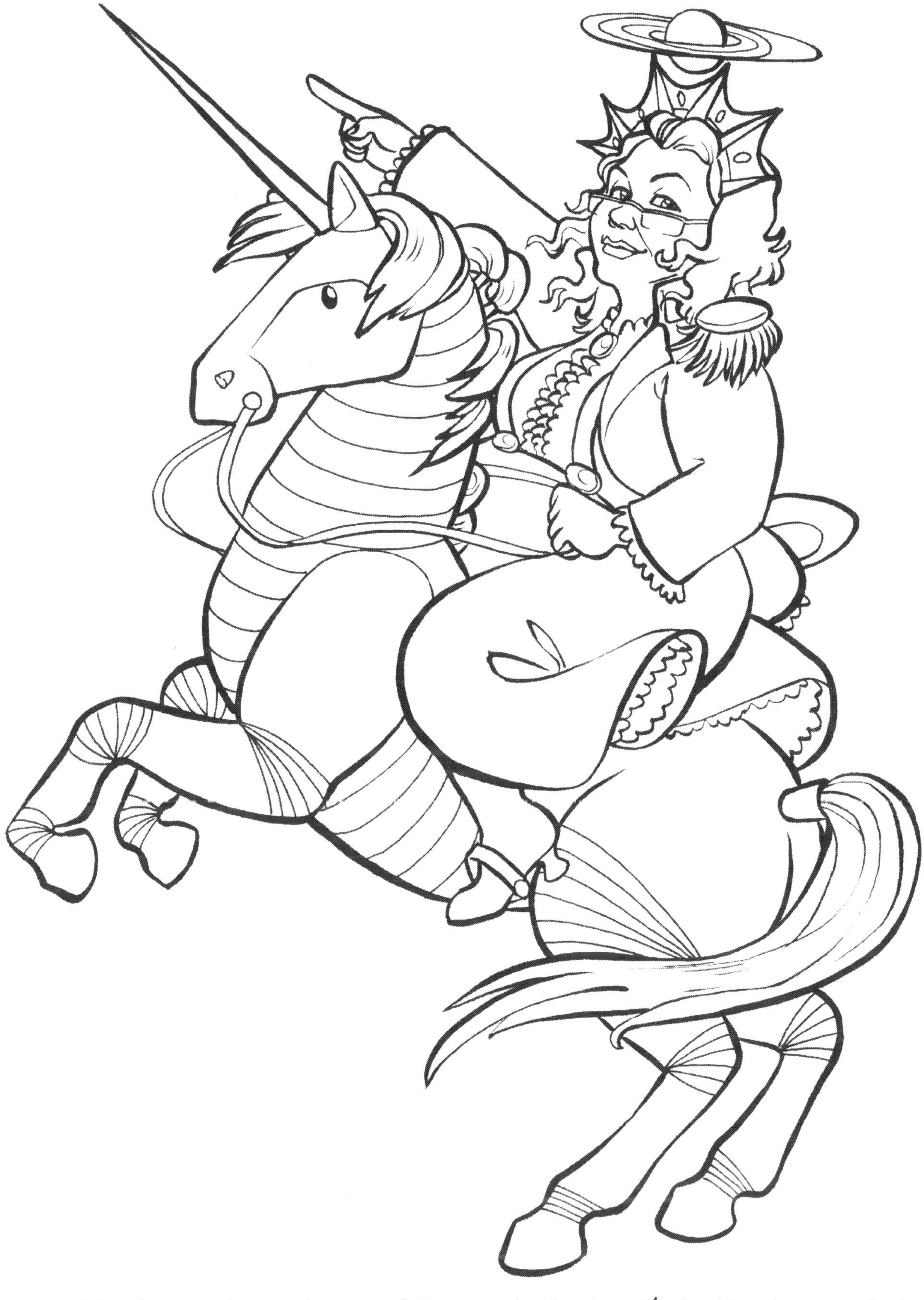

Princess Marianne has charged her robot steed's batteries and donned her questing tiara. Somewhere in her kingdom, adventure awaits!

About this book

The idea for Fat Ladies in Spaaaaace came from a panel at WisCon 34, when one panelist asked, "Why are there no fat butches in space?" Nicole started sketching, and Sincerity was inked by the end of the next panel. After that, peer pressure did the rest.

Five fantastic women modeled for fat sci-fi heroines in this book: Wendy (The Zaftig Zephyr), Kirstine (Dr. Frk), Becca (Bec), Bex (Diva), and Marianne (Princess Marianne).

About the Artist

Nicole is an artist and fantasy writer living in Saint Paul, Minnesota. Her inner child is pretty psyched about this coloring book thing.

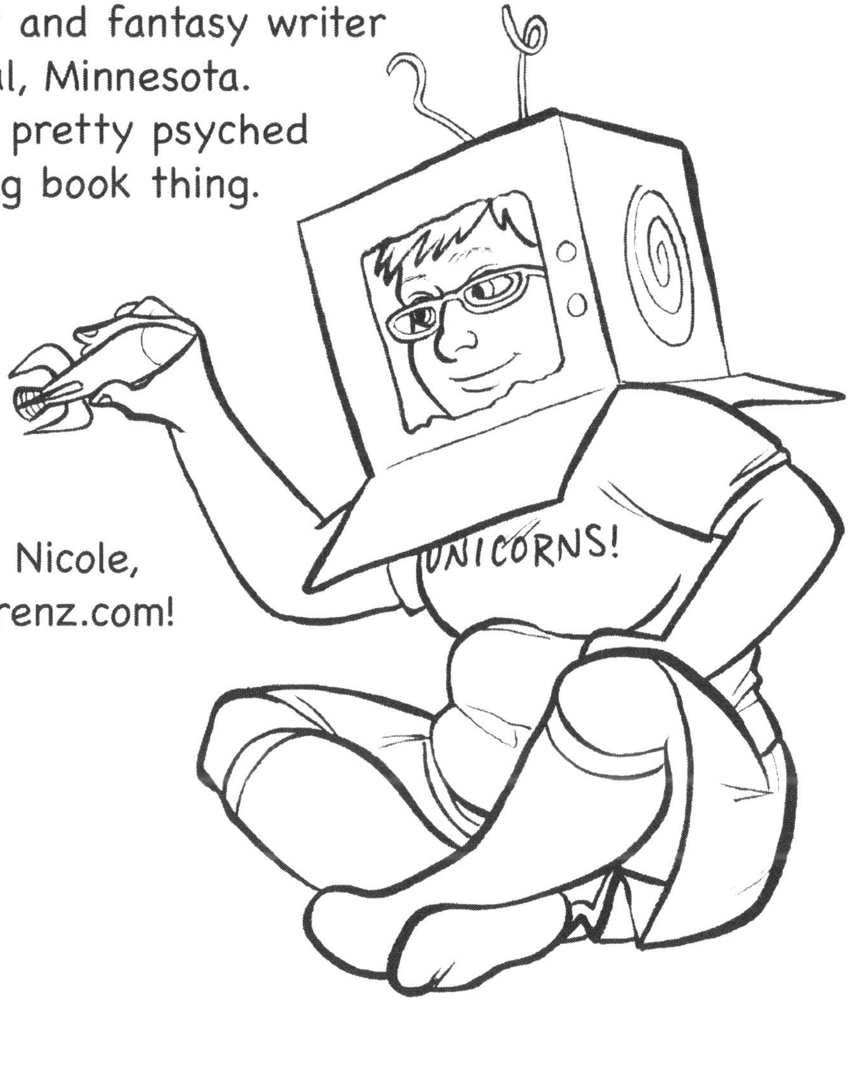
UNICORNS!

For more stuff by Nicole, visit www.nicolelorenz.com!

Made in the USA
San Bernardino, CA
17 October 2015